IT'S TIME TO EAT GREEN OLIVES

It's Time to Eat
GREEN OLIVES

Walter the Educator

Silent King Books
A WhichHead Entertainment Imprint

Copyright © 2025 by Walter the Educator

All rights reserved. No part of this book may be reproduced in any manner whatsoever without written per- mission except in the case of brief quotations embodied in critical articles and reviews.

First Printing, 2024

Disclaimer

This book is a literary work; the story is not about specific persons, locations, situations, and/or circumstances unless mentioned in a historical context. Any resemblance to real persons, locations, situations, and/or circumstances is coincidental. This book is for entertainment and informational purposes only. The author and publisher offer this information without warranties expressed or implied. No matter the grounds, neither the author nor the publisher will be accountable for any losses, injuries, or other damages caused by the reader's use of this book. The use of this book acknowledges an understanding and acceptance of this disclaimer.

It's Time to Eat GREEN OLIVES is a collectible early learning book by Walter the Educator suitable for all ages belonging to Walter the Educator's Time to Eat Book Series. Collect more books at WaltertheEducator.com

USE THE EXTRA SPACE TO TAKE NOTES AND DOCUMENT YOUR MEMORIES

GREEN OLIVES

It's time to eat, come take a seat!

It's Time to Eat
Green Olives

A little snack, so fun to eat!

Round and shiny, small and bright,

Green olives are a tasty bite!

Some are big and some are small,

Some are stuffed and some are tall!

Some are salty, some are sweet,

Green olives are a special treat!

Pop one in and have a try,

Taste so tangy, oh my, oh my!

A little bitter, smooth and new,

Green olives have a flavor true!

Stack them high or eat them plain,

On a sandwich or a grain!

Toss them fresh into a spread,

Or on pizza, nice and red!

It's Time to Eat
Green Olives

Crunch and munch, then have some more,

A jar of olives to explore!

Pits inside? Just take it slow,

Chew with care, now off you go!

In a salad, on a dish,

Green olives grant your every wish!

Pair with cheese or eat with bread,

A tasty treat from A to Zed!

Do you like them soft or firm?

Eat them once, and you'll return!

Try them cold or try them warm,

Olives come in every form!

Did you know they grow on trees?

Swaying gently in the breeze!

Picked and brined for all to share,

It's Time to Eat
Green
Olives

A yummy food beyond compare!

Take a bite and you will see,

Olives are so good for me!

Salty, yummy, soft, and round,

A perfect snack that can be found!

So grab some now, don't wait too late,

Time to eat, oh, it's so great!

Green and tasty, one, two, three,

It's Time to Eat Green Olives

Eating olives, yay for me!

ABOUT THE CREATOR

Walter the Educator is one of the pseudonyms for Walter Anderson. Formally educated in Chemistry, Business, and Education, he is an educator, an author, a diverse entrepreneur, and he is the son of a disabled war veteran. "Walter the Educator" shares his time between educating and creating. He holds interests and owns several creative projects that entertain, enlighten, enhance, and educate, hoping to inspire and motivate you. Follow, find new works, and stay up to date with Walter the Educator™

at WaltertheEducator.com

www.ingramcontent.com/pod-product-compliance
Lightning Source LLC
LaVergne TN
LVHW010623070526
838199LV00063BA/5251